SEAS THE DAY
A year of sea swimming poetry

Rachael Boughton

INTRODUCTION

I grew up in Dorset and spent many summers swimming in the Sea at West Bay as a child. We had a sailing boat, and I still remember the sense of escapism as we left the shore behind; nothing but the Sea between me and the horizon.

But from September onwards there was a sort of unspoken rule about the Sea. That this was a time when the beach should be for windswept walks, and the wild Sea should be observed from a safe (warm!) distance.

Little did I know that many years later the world would experience a global pandemic that would enforce a lockdown on our lives. It was during this time that I found myself beside the water's edge; inexplicably drawn to the Sea, in search of something that could release me.

From the moment I entered the cold water I experienced something transformational; a sense of freedom and peace, all worries left behind on the shore. I returned over and over, to throw my inner wild child into the Sea with sheer abandon. It was this fleeting freedom from the restrictions of life that nourished my soul and fostered my resilience during such a difficult time. It now continues to give me the strength and courage to take on many other challenges in life.

But more than this; the Sea helped me to rediscover a love of words. This act of cold-water ritual has had such a profound effect on me; I am driven to respond to it, to speak of it, write about it, and share it. It has unlocked a language of wild words within me. A language spoken by wild souls, one that has been whispered on the wind, and carried across the water from a time long ago. A time when perhaps we were all wild and free.

The poems in this book are my love letters to the Sea. They are written shortly after each swim and, along with extracts from my journal at the time, these words are an attempt to set the scene, to tell you a story, to invoke the magic brought about by each swim. There were many more swims throughout the year, but the ones featured in this book are the ones that truly spoke to me.

Due to Covid travel restrictions the majority of swims took place at the same beach at West Bay. It still intrigues me how, despite the same location, the Sea is ever-changing and no swim is ever the same. The photographs, all taken at the time of the swim, offer a visual perspective.

As such, you are invited into the very moment each swim took place; to hear the story, and to share the experience. Perhaps it will resonate with you, perhaps it will inspire you, above all my hope is that it might speak to you of the magic that can happen in cold water, and the powerful effect that the natural world can bestow upon us.

SEAS THE DAY

JANUARY

"The mornings are cold and dark and yet I am leaving the warmth of my bed to get up, make a flask of coffee, scrape the ice from the windscreen and head to the beach in my swimwear. What madness is this!? I swam with Ginny & Mel this morning. We met at dawn and swam in the ocean as the sun rose up over the Isle of Portland."

We rose before the sun.
Sleep still clinging to our skin.
Peeling away the warmth of our clothes,
we enter the cold with a gasp. Then...
Eyes bright.
Heart bursting with life!
There in the ocean, awaiting the light,
the sun is a promise beholden to night.
The dawn giving hope, while stars are still bright.
Beneath this vast sky, adrift from the shore,
there's a sense of adventure, so much *more* to explore.
I'm carried by water, the ebb of the wave.
This is my "why".
This is my "brave".

A year of sea swimming poetry

SWIMRISE WEST BAY, DORSET

FEBRUARY

"I've learned that the full moon in February goes by the name of the Snow Moon. With a clear sky and light wind, I met with fellow swimmers on the beach last night. I watched the moon rise from behind East Cliff while swimming in the ocean. It could only have been more magical if it had snowed. It gave me an entirely different perspective on a view I thought I'd known all my life!."

We swam by the light of the moon last night,
in the sea reflecting its beam.
Rising bright and full,
the tide in its pull,
We bathed in a magical dream.
There were stars in the sky, clear as crystal last night,
as we dressed on the moonlit beach.
Boosted in spirit,
and all that came with it,
the Snow Moon and what it could teach.
"We swam by the light of the moon last night",
I whisper to the rising sun.
But the world just turns,
and the sun, she burns,
for this is life.
This is how it is done.

A year of sea swimming poetry

MOON RISING WEST BAY, DORSET

MARCH

"The weather in spring is known for being changeable; a little of this, and a little of that. But swimming out there in the ocean, with the sunny spells and the rain showers all at once, it really heightens this sense of awareness. By noticing the changes, it is focusing on the things we so easily take for granted. It is becoming a form of mindfulness."

Shining silver sea beneath roaming rolling clouds.
The rays of sunshine, always just out of reach.
Warm wind in our faces.
We swim between scattered showers.
Droplets of rain, like tiny diamonds pierce the surface.
Spring is a temptress.
She promises warmth.
Enticing us to wear less, feel lighter...
Then, as the music changes,
she laughs.
She dances away to a different tune...
Leaving us bewitched, bemused and bewildered.

A year of sea swimming poetry

BRIDPORT BLUETITS WEST BAY, DORSET

SEAS THE DAY

APRIL

"Another full moon swim, this time the Pink Moon (reputedly named after the blossom at this time of year). With the moon reaching the closest point in orbit to the earth at this time of year it also appears much larger than usual. I swam with the Bridport Bluetits at West Bay. The sun was setting in the west while the Pink Moon was rising in the east. As we swam between the two, we didn't know which way to look. We were quite breathless!"

As we gather on the shore,
we stand around and gaze in awe.
While sinking sun and rising moon,
perform a dance to nature's tune.
The sea a stage, a scene, a part.
Reflecting colours like fine art.
With beating hearts and trembling limbs,
we brave the waves, as daylight dims.
But what is this!? Oh sunset bliss,
the water's surface has been kissed!
With reds, and orange, mauve and pinks,
our skin aglow, as sunlight sinks.
And as we turn, we howl with glee,
the full moon hangs above the sea.
We wonder how the tides of time,
have danced this tune, and know this rhyme.
And so, as we return to shore,
enchanted still by what we saw,
we smile and shiver in harmony.
T'was a magical night of lunar-sea.

A year of sea swimming poetry

SUNSET WEST BAY, DORSET

SEAS THE DAY

MAY

"The warmer weather in May seems to bring with it an invitation to get out and explore. Today we took the children to Tyneham Village & Worbarrow Bay. I remember going there when I was a child. It was so inspiring to get out and see the landscape through their eyes. It felt like a magical adventure, like the setting for an Enid Blyton story. In the spirit of adventure, I couldn't resist having an impromptu swim!"

We explored along the Dorset coast,
kids and dogs and a camping stove.
Salty wind and spells of sun,
our hearts set sail on a trail of fun.
Wooded valleys and windswept cliffs
no sense of time, just free, such bliss!
Then there before us, as the tide drew back,
lay a secret cove full of jagged cracks.
We cooked upon a wood smoke fire,
and bellies full, we soon grew tired.
Like lazy lizards on warm stone,
we lay a while with sea bird's moans.
Then curiosity tugged our feet,
the rocks and caves, a hidden treat.
The dogs are hunting as we go.
The feel of stone beneath our toes.
A primal sense of wilder times,
we live to learn, we seek, we find.
And so, when it is time to leave
our hearts are full, and I believe,
that nature is our state of mind.
We came to seek, and we did find.

A year of sea swimming poetry

ADVENTURES WORBARROW BAY, DORSET

SEAS THE DAY

JUNE

"I have discovered that River swimming is a welcome relief from the blazing heat and crowds at the beach. It is so serene and tranquil. The shade of the trees, the gentle sound of water flowing and the smell of damp earth. It was such a change from the salt and sand of the Sea – it had a totally different energy."

I walked in the hot summer sun
to the cool shade of the woodland.
Baked earth beneath my feet,
warm air on my bare skin.
Dappled sunlight falling around me like delicate gold leaf.
I stand a while, eyes closed, heart open.
There you are.
I hear you.
River running like freedom flowing, your sound seeps into my soul...
I follow.
Senses keen.
Arriving at the water's edge.
An elemental meeting of water, air and earth,
beneath the fire of the June sun, and the joy in my heart.
As I enter the water, I stumble.
Current tugging at my waist,
I surrender to the flow.
Take me there...

And held by the power of nature,
I gaze up at the emerald canopy of the ancient trees.
I gently float down river.
Soul quenched.

A year of sea swimming poetry

RIVER SWIM

SEAS THE DAY

JULY

"These morning swims are becoming something of a ritual for me in these last weeks of term!. After the chaos of the morning school-run, I am relieved to get to the beach, to meet my kindred spirits as we dive into the ocean. It's the perfect way to wake up properly and fully embrace the day. A chance to refresh in time for the summer holidays".

With dust of sleep still in my eyes,
And dreams forgotten by sunrise,
I wave farewell to my sweet boy,
Amidst the bags and playground noise.
The sea is calling, clear and bright.
A summer morning blue delight.
With kindred spirits on the beach,
We meet and speak of struggles each.
And as we walk to greet the waves,
The smiles return, we find our brave.
We laugh within the salt and swell.
The rush of cold wakes every cell.
Alive with every breath we take,
How good it feels to be awake.
To see the light, no longer dim.
Oh, how I LOVE the morning swim!

A year of sea swimming poetry

KINDRED SPIRITS WEST BAY, DORSET

SEAS THE DAY

AUGUST

"The beaches are SO busy with tourists. Early swims are now a firm favourite. I arrived at 6:30am this morning and footprints revealed that others had been before me... I smiled as I wondered who had left them? I would definitely know some of these wild souls. It prompted me to write a poem BEFORE my swim today. I wanted to capture the mystery (and not include my own footprints in the scene)."

Footprints.
Sunken shapes in the sand.
Impressing upon the shore.
A tale of morning pilgrimage.
Of barefoot journeys to the water's edge.
Invisible beings, ghost walkers.
Alone or gathered, one by one, side by side.
Willing to be taken.
To be swept away,
In the divine act of cold-water ritual.
Leaving nothing of their former selves but,
Soft shadows, left among the shells.
Each one a silent statement.
A signature of a wild soul.

A year of sea swimming poetry

FOOTPRINTS WEST BAY, DORSET

SEPTEMBER

"Durdle Door is considered to be the "jewel in the crown" of our Jurassic Coast. It's not far from West Bay, but the traffic and crowds put me off going in summer. I've been waiting for it to become a little quieter - and today was the day! With most people back at work and school, and an unexpected heat wave, I made a last-minute decision to go. It was (as I knew it would be) worth the wait."

The last days of summer cling,
like delicate tendrils wound around bare feet.
A quietness falls on the morning mists,
as cool dawn air mingles with mellow sun.
It is time...

I walk.
On soft white chalk,
a salty path of powdered dust,
to climb the cliff.
To stop and stare with bated breath.
To greet you.
You rise from the ocean floor,
arching tall, all jagged rock and cutting crescent.
Like the moon, no single glance can suffice.
Oh! how I've waited!
A long feverish summer,
while madding crowds,
flocked to dance upon these rocks.
Yet still, I held my breath.
Waiting my tender turn.
'Til now, here.
And in the space that surrounds us,
I breathe again.
As the last days of summer gently release me,
kissing the silky surface of the sea,
I descend.
Sinking deep into the quiet blue.
Submerged in silence.
In a sea of awe.
To swim wild and free,
through the Durdle Door.

A year of sea swimming poetry

LAST DAYS OF SUMMER DURDLE DOOR, DORSET

OCTOBER

"The weather is really turning now and the storms have been letting us know autumn has arrived. With the high winds and wild waves lately, there has been no chance of swimming. But after a few days of watching and waiting I finally went for a swim with the Bridport Bluetits. This enforced absence from the water has been a valuable opportunity; to consider how powerful nature is, and to be mindful to take notice, and respect it."

In the wake of the storm there lies understanding,
that nature has fought and has won.
Her rage, an assault, a riot resounding,
relentless until it is done.
As we wake from the storm to find all is now quiet,
we forgive but we must not forget.
That life can be fragile, with battles SO fierce,
we must live it, with no regret.
Take a note of the lessons we're given to learn,
understand that the world can change.
Seas the day, while you can,
we can all take our turn,
to rejoice in the sun, after rain.

A year of sea swimming poetry

AFTER THE STORM, WEST BAY, DORSET
CREDIT: JANE MALCOLM

SEAS THE DAY

NOVEMBER

"It is a mad rush to get changed and warm after swimming at the moment. The temperature in the water is several degrees warmer than the air temperature. "The hard bit isn't getting in, it's getting out!" I heard someone say. And in this frantic scrabble to get dressed, all numb fingers and brain fog, it is easy to turn your back on the Sea and forget her. To selfishly take what we want, and move on. But I took a moment to "land" after this morning's swim. Once dressed, I returned to the shore to give thanks to the Sea and all that she gave me."

The reflective moment after a swim.
Appreciating the water, and all that it gave me.
Accepting its indifference to me and all that surrounds it.
Knowing it will continue to ebb and flow without me, regardless.
Tides will turn, sun and moon will rise and set,
seasons will dance around it;
Winds teasing, temperatures freezing, storms seizing.
I am its witness.
I came, I saw, I became so much more.
A mind released.
Immersed in the Sea.
I was with you, a while,
I was wild and free.

A year of sea swimming poetry

REFLECTION WEST BAY, DORSET

DECEMBER

"My first Christmas morning swim! Swimmers arrived at dawn to greet the day, and there was a definite sense of celebration in the air as the sky began to change colour. I made driftwood gifts and left them by the pier for whoever might find them; a message burnt into the wood that said "Seas The Day". As we swam, Jim a local musician, arrived on the shore with his trumpet. He played "Silent Night" for his partner Sammy as she swam. To float in the ocean, while the music was carried from shore to sky, felt like a truly unique gift!"

What greater gift can Winter bring,
than meeting for a festive swim.
With kin who gather round to share,
a fellowship for Those That Dare.
With treasures left beneath the pier,
"there's one for me!", I hear a cheer.
With song and laughter ringing out,
across the water, as we shout,
warm greetings made of tide and joy,
with noses pink as bobbing buoys.
And as the sunrise takes our gaze,
upon the shore a trumpet plays!
The dreamy notes of "Silent Night",
to thank the stars for shining bright.
For now its time to "Seas The Day".
To celebrate a wilder way.
With nature as the greatest host.
To give the gift that matters most.
To know there is no better worth,
than feeling grateful for this earth.
And so it is with beating hearts,
we bid farewells, as we depart.
Glad for all that we have shared.
The festive swim, for Those That Dared.

A year of sea swimming poetry

CHRISTMAS MORNING WEST BAY, DORSET

SEAS THE DAY DRIFTWOOD GIFT

SEAS THE DAY

10% OF PROFITS DONATED TO MENTAL HEALTH SWIMS

Mental Health Swims is an award-winning, mental health peer support community. They host free, safe and inclusive swim meet ups nationwide, open to all. Participants can swim, dip, paddle or toe-dip and can do what they are most comfortable with. Swims are firmly focused on dips, not distance and community, not competition.

My journey into the water has been a game changer in terms of managing my CPTSD. However I doubt I would have continued swimming through the winter without first attending a Mental Health Swim hosted by Tess Kelly (Dorset Dips).

The mental health benefits of cold water immersion is widely documented, however it can be daunting to stand at the water's edge alone. Aside from the obvious risks of swimming solo, it takes a lot of motivation to get into the cold water on a grey morning in January! Swimming with MHS can make it fun, supported and safe to do so. It is for this reason that I am donating 10% of profits from the sale of this book to support Mental Health Swims in the work they do to make it accessible to all.

www.mentalhealthswims.co.uk

BOOK COVER ARTWORK

The beautiful linocut on the cover was commissioned especially for this book and is by Prints By The Bay.

Prints by the Bay is the printmaking practice of Nicole Purdie, a professional linocut illustrator based on the Dorset coast. Her work is female centric, containing strong visual narratives and storytelling which examines connections between people and place. Much of her work explores the human condition, with an emphasis on the importance of our connection to earth and nature.

www.printsbythebay.com

Instagram/Facebook: @printsbythebay

A year of sea swimming poetry

SPECIAL THANKS

I have met so many inspiring people on my journey into the Sea. It's been like joining a tribe of wild souls! Here are some of those lovely people; The Bridport Bluetits (far too many to mention but you are all amazing!) Erin, Jodi, Tess Kelly (Dorset Dips), Mental Health Swims, Sarah (Seaside Sauna Haus), Simon Jordan, Swimzine and all the #wildswimming folk I've connected with online!

Cold water swimming doesn't come without risk and while every care is taken to stay safe and be aware of the sea conditions, there will always be an element of danger when you are subjecting yourself to a powerful body of water. It is for this reason I give thanks to our local RNLI in Lyme Regis who commit to saving lives at sea on the Jurassic Coast.

Last but by no means least, I must thank my husband Roly and our two boys (Jed and Isaac) who have helped me put this book together. Most importantly, they never grumble when they wake to find I have disappeared off for a dawn swim, again!

SEAS THE DAY